THIS BOOK BELONGS TO:

CONTACT INFORMATION

NAME:	
ADDRESS:	
PHONE:	

START / END DATES

/ /   TO   / /

DEDICATION

This Meditation Journal log is dedicated to all the people out there who love meditating or want to start, and document their findings in the process.

You are my inspiration for producing books and I'm honored to be a part of keeping all of your meditation notes and records organized.

This journal notebook will help you record your details about your meditations.

Thoughtfully put together with these sections to record in detail: Data & Time, How Long, Mood Tracker, Thoughts/ Notes, Sleep Tracker, Self-Care Tracker, & Daily Journal.

HOW TO USE THIS BOOK

The purpose of this book is to keep all of your Meditation notes all in one place. It will help keep you organized.

This Meditation Journal will allow you to accurately document every detail about your meditation experience. It's a great way to chart your course through daily meditation.

Here are examples of the prompts for you to fill in and write about your experience in this book:

1. Date & Time - Write the time, month, day, and year.

2. How Long - Log how long you meditated.

3. Mood Tracker - Record how you felt before & after meditation, good, neutral, or stressed.

4. Thoughts/ Notes - Write any specific thoughts that came to mind while meditating.

5. Sleep Tracker - Log sleep quality, hours you slept, what time you went to bed, & dream notes.

6. Self Care Tracker - Record your mind and spirit health at the moment, along with any physical activity or exercise.

7. Daily Journal - Write any other important detail about your day that you like, such as your main focus, positive affirmations, personal thoughts, inspirational quotes, creative ideas, goals, special prayer for the day, etc.

MEDITATION LOG

DATE		TIME		HOW LONG	

MOOD TRACKER:

BEFORE	AFTER	THOUGHTS / NOTES ON YOUR MEDITATION
☐ GOOD	☐ GOOD	
☐ NEUTRAL	☐ NEUTRAL	
☐ STRESSED	☐ STRESSED	

SLEEP TRACKER:

SLEEP QUALITY	HOW MANY HOURS DID YOU SLEEP?	DREAM NOTES
☐ GOOD		
☐ NEUTRAL	WHAT TIME DID YOU GO TO BED?	
☐ STRESSED	☐ AM ☐ PM	

SELF CARE TRACKER:

MIND / SPIRIT	EXERCISE / PHYSICAL ACTIVITY

DAILY JOURNAL

MEDITATION LOG

DATE	TIME	HOW LONG

MOOD TRACKER:

BEFORE	AFTER	THOUGHTS / NOTES ON YOUR MEDITATION
☐ GOOD	☐ GOOD	
☐ NEUTRAL	☐ NEUTRAL	
☐ STRESSED	☐ STRESSED	

SLEEP TRACKER:

SLEEP QUALITY	HOW MANY HOURS DID YOU SLEEP?	DREAM NOTES
☐ GOOD		
☐ NEUTRAL	WHAT TIME DID YOU GO TO BED?	
☐ STRESSED	☐ AM ☐ PM	

SELF CARE TRACKER:

MIND / SPIRIT	EXERCISE / PHYSICAL ACTIVITY

DAILY JOURNAL

MEDITATION LOG

DATE		TIME		HOW LONG	

MOOD TRACKER:

BEFORE	AFTER	THOUGHTS / NOTES ON YOUR MEDITATION
☐ GOOD	☐ GOOD	
☐ NEUTRAL	☐ NEUTRAL	
☐ STRESSED	☐ STRESSED	

SLEEP TRACKER:

SLEEP QUALITY	HOW MANY HOURS DID YOU SLEEP?	DREAM NOTES
☐ GOOD		
☐ NEUTRAL	WHAT TIME DID YOU GO TO BED?	
☐ STRESSED	☐ AM ☐ PM	

SELF CARE TRACKER:

MIND / SPIRIT	EXERCISE / PHYSICAL ACTIVITY

DAILY JOURNAL

MEDITATION LOG

DATE	TIME	HOW LONG

MOOD TRACKER:

BEFORE	AFTER	THOUGHTS / NOTES ON YOUR MEDITATION
☐ GOOD	☐ GOOD	
☐ NEUTRAL	☐ NEUTRAL	
☐ STRESSED	☐ STRESSED	

SLEEP TRACKER:

SLEEP QUALITY	HOW MANY HOURS DID YOU SLEEP?	DREAM NOTES
☐ GOOD		
☐ NEUTRAL	WHAT TIME DID YOU GO TO BED?	
☐ STRESSED	☐ AM ☐ PM	

SELF CARE TRACKER:

MIND / SPIRIT	EXERCISE / PHYSICAL ACTIVITY

DAILY JOURNAL

MEDITATION LOG

DATE	TIME	HOW LONG

MOOD TRACKER:

BEFORE	AFTER	THOUGHTS / NOTES ON YOUR MEDITATION
☐ GOOD	☐ GOOD	
☐ NEUTRAL	☐ NEUTRAL	
☐ STRESSED	☐ STRESSED	

SLEEP TRACKER:

SLEEP QUALITY	HOW MANY HOURS DID YOU SLEEP?	DREAM NOTES
☐ GOOD		
☐ NEUTRAL	WHAT TIME DID YOU GO TO BED?	
☐ STRESSED	☐ AM ☐ PM	

SELF CARE TRACKER:

MIND / SPIRIT	EXERCISE / PHYSICAL ACTIVITY

DAILY JOURNAL

MEDITATION LOG

DATE	TIME	HOW LONG

MOOD TRACKER:

BEFORE	AFTER	THOUGHTS / NOTES ON YOUR MEDITATION
☐ GOOD	☐ GOOD	
☐ NEUTRAL	☐ NEUTRAL	
☐ STRESSED	☐ STRESSED	

SLEEP TRACKER:

SLEEP QUALITY	HOW MANY HOURS DID YOU SLEEP?	DREAM NOTES
☐ GOOD		
☐ NEUTRAL	WHAT TIME DID YOU GO TO BED?	
☐ STRESSED	☐ AM ☐ PM	

SELF CARE TRACKER:

MIND / SPIRIT	EXERCISE / PHYSICAL ACTIVITY

DAILY JOURNAL

MEDITATION LOG

DATE		TIME		HOW LONG	

MOOD TRACKER:

BEFORE	AFTER	THOUGHTS / NOTES ON YOUR MEDITATION
☐ GOOD	☐ GOOD	
☐ NEUTRAL	☐ NEUTRAL	
☐ STRESSED	☐ STRESSED	

SLEEP TRACKER:

SLEEP QUALITY	HOW MANY HOURS DID YOU SLEEP?	DREAM NOTES
☐ GOOD		
☐ NEUTRAL	WHAT TIME DID YOU GO TO BED?	
☐ STRESSED	☐ AM ☐ PM	

SELF CARE TRACKER:

MIND / SPIRIT	EXERCISE / PHYSICAL ACTIVITY

DAILY JOURNAL

MEDITATION LOG

DATE	TIME	HOW LONG

MOOD TRACKER:

BEFORE	AFTER	THOUGHTS / NOTES ON YOUR MEDITATION
☐ GOOD	☐ GOOD	
☐ NEUTRAL	☐ NEUTRAL	
☐ STRESSED	☐ STRESSED	

SLEEP TRACKER:

SLEEP QUALITY	HOW MANY HOURS DID YOU SLEEP?	DREAM NOTES
☐ GOOD		
☐ NEUTRAL	WHAT TIME DID YOU GO TO BED?	
☐ STRESSED	☐ AM ☐ PM	

SELF CARE TRACKER:

MIND / SPIRIT	EXERCISE / PHYSICAL ACTIVITY

DAILY JOURNAL

MEDITATION LOG

DATE	TIME	HOW LONG

MOOD TRACKER:

BEFORE	AFTER	THOUGHTS / NOTES ON YOUR MEDITATION
☐ GOOD	☐ GOOD	
☐ NEUTRAL	☐ NEUTRAL	
☐ STRESSED	☐ STRESSED	

SLEEP TRACKER:

SLEEP QUALITY	HOW MANY HOURS DID YOU SLEEP?	DREAM NOTES
☐ GOOD		
☐ NEUTRAL	WHAT TIME DID YOU GO TO BED?	
☐ STRESSED	☐ AM ☐ PM	

SELF CARE TRACKER:

MIND / SPIRIT	EXERCISE / PHYSICAL ACTIVITY

DAILY JOURNAL

MEDITATION LOG

DATE   TIME   HOW LONG

MOOD TRACKER:

BEFORE	AFTER	THOUGHTS / NOTES ON YOUR MEDITATION
☐ GOOD	☐ GOOD	
☐ NEUTRAL	☐ NEUTRAL	
☐ STRESSED	☐ STRESSED	

SLEEP TRACKER:

SLEEP QUALITY	HOW MANY HOURS DID YOU SLEEP?	DREAM NOTES
☐ GOOD		
☐ NEUTRAL	WHAT TIME DID YOU GO TO BED?	
☐ STRESSED	☐ AM ☐ PM	

SELF CARE TRACKER:

MIND / SPIRIT	EXERCISE / PHYSICAL ACTIVITY

DAILY JOURNAL

MEDITATION LOG

DATE		TIME		HOW LONG	

MOOD TRACKER:

BEFORE	AFTER	THOUGHTS / NOTES ON YOUR MEDITATION
☐ GOOD	☐ GOOD	
☐ NEUTRAL	☐ NEUTRAL	
☐ STRESSED	☐ STRESSED	

SLEEP TRACKER:

SLEEP QUALITY	HOW MANY HOURS DID YOU SLEEP?	DREAM NOTES
☐ GOOD		
☐ NEUTRAL	WHAT TIME DID YOU GO TO BED?	
☐ STRESSED	☐ AM ☐ PM	

SELF CARE TRACKER:

MIND / SPIRIT	EXERCISE / PHYSICAL ACTIVITY

DAILY JOURNAL

MEDITATION LOG

DATE	TIME	HOW LONG

MOOD TRACKER:

BEFORE	AFTER	THOUGHTS / NOTES ON YOUR MEDITATION
☐ GOOD	☐ GOOD	
☐ NEUTRAL	☐ NEUTRAL	
☐ STRESSED	☐ STRESSED	

SLEEP TRACKER:

SLEEP QUALITY	HOW MANY HOURS DID YOU SLEEP?	DREAM NOTES
☐ GOOD		
☐ NEUTRAL	WHAT TIME DID YOU GO TO BED?	
☐ STRESSED	☐ AM ☐ PM	

SELF CARE TRACKER:

MIND / SPIRIT	EXERCISE / PHYSICAL ACTIVITY

DAILY JOURNAL

MEDITATION LOG

DATE	TIME	HOW LONG

MOOD TRACKER:

BEFORE	AFTER	THOUGHTS / NOTES ON YOUR MEDITATION
☐ GOOD	☐ GOOD	
☐ NEUTRAL	☐ NEUTRAL	
☐ STRESSED	☐ STRESSED	

SLEEP TRACKER:

SLEEP QUALITY	HOW MANY HOURS DID YOU SLEEP?	DREAM NOTES
☐ GOOD		
☐ NEUTRAL	WHAT TIME DID YOU GO TO BED?	
☐ STRESSED	☐ AM ☐ PM	

SELF CARE TRACKER:

MIND / SPIRIT	EXERCISE / PHYSICAL ACTIVITY

DAILY JOURNAL

MEDITATION LOG

DATE	TIME	HOW LONG

MOOD TRACKER:

BEFORE	AFTER	THOUGHTS / NOTES ON YOUR MEDITATION
☐ GOOD	☐ GOOD	
☐ NEUTRAL	☐ NEUTRAL	
☐ STRESSED	☐ STRESSED	

SLEEP TRACKER:

SLEEP QUALITY	HOW MANY HOURS DID YOU SLEEP?	DREAM NOTES
☐ GOOD		
☐ NEUTRAL	WHAT TIME DID YOU GO TO BED?	
☐ STRESSED	☐ AM ☐ PM	

SELF CARE TRACKER:

MIND / SPIRIT	EXERCISE / PHYSICAL ACTIVITY

DAILY JOURNAL

MEDITATION LOG

DATE		TIME	HOW LONG

MOOD TRACKER:

BEFORE	AFTER	THOUGHTS / NOTES ON YOUR MEDITATION
☐ GOOD	☐ GOOD	
☐ NEUTRAL	☐ NEUTRAL	
☐ STRESSED	☐ STRESSED	

SLEEP TRACKER:

SLEEP QUALITY	HOW MANY HOURS DID YOU SLEEP?	DREAM NOTES
☐ GOOD		
☐ NEUTRAL	WHAT TIME DID YOU GO TO BED?	
☐ STRESSED	☐ AM ☐ PM	

SELF CARE TRACKER:

MIND / SPIRIT	EXERCISE / PHYSICAL ACTIVITY

DAILY JOURNAL

MEDITATION LOG

DATE	TIME	HOW LONG

MOOD TRACKER:

BEFORE	AFTER	THOUGHTS / NOTES ON YOUR MEDITATION
☐ GOOD	☐ GOOD	
☐ NEUTRAL	☐ NEUTRAL	
☐ STRESSED	☐ STRESSED	

SLEEP TRACKER:

SLEEP QUALITY	HOW MANY HOURS DID YOU SLEEP?	DREAM NOTES
☐ GOOD		
☐ NEUTRAL	WHAT TIME DID YOU GO TO BED?	
☐ STRESSED	☐ AM ☐ PM	

SELF CARE TRACKER:

MIND / SPIRIT	EXERCISE / PHYSICAL ACTIVITY

DAILY JOURNAL

MEDITATION LOG

DATE		TIME		HOW LONG	

MOOD TRACKER:

BEFORE	AFTER	THOUGHTS / NOTES ON YOUR MEDITATION
☐ GOOD	☐ GOOD	
☐ NEUTRAL	☐ NEUTRAL	
☐ STRESSED	☐ STRESSED	

SLEEP TRACKER:

SLEEP QUALITY	HOW MANY HOURS DID YOU SLEEP?	DREAM NOTES
☐ GOOD		
☐ NEUTRAL	WHAT TIME DID YOU GO TO BED?	
☐ STRESSED	☐ AM ☐ PM	

SELF CARE TRACKER:

MIND / SPIRIT	EXERCISE / PHYSICAL ACTIVITY

DAILY JOURNAL

MEDITATION LOG

DATE	TIME	HOW LONG

MOOD TRACKER:

BEFORE	AFTER	THOUGHTS / NOTES ON YOUR MEDITATION
☐ GOOD	☐ GOOD	
☐ NEUTRAL	☐ NEUTRAL	
☐ STRESSED	☐ STRESSED	

SLEEP TRACKER:

SLEEP QUALITY	HOW MANY HOURS DID YOU SLEEP?	DREAM NOTES
☐ GOOD		
☐ NEUTRAL	WHAT TIME DID YOU GO TO BED?	
☐ STRESSED	☐ AM ☐ PM	

SELF CARE TRACKER:

MIND / SPIRIT	EXERCISE / PHYSICAL ACTIVITY

DAILY JOURNAL

MEDITATION LOG

DATE	TIME	HOW LONG

MOOD TRACKER:

BEFORE	AFTER		THOUGHTS / NOTES ON YOUR MEDITATION
☐ GOOD	☐ GOOD		
☐ NEUTRAL	☐ NEUTRAL		
☐ STRESSED	☐ STRESSED		

SLEEP TRACKER:

SLEEP QUALITY	HOW MANY HOURS DID YOU SLEEP?		DREAM NOTES
☐ GOOD			
☐ NEUTRAL	WHAT TIME DID YOU GO TO BED?		
☐ STRESSED		☐ AM ☐ PM	

SELF CARE TRACKER:

MIND / SPIRIT	EXERCISE / PHYSICAL ACTIVITY

DAILY JOURNAL

MEDITATION LOG

DATE	TIME	HOW LONG

MOOD TRACKER:

BEFORE	AFTER	THOUGHTS / NOTES ON YOUR MEDITATION
☐ GOOD	☐ GOOD	
☐ NEUTRAL	☐ NEUTRAL	
☐ STRESSED	☐ STRESSED	

SLEEP TRACKER:

SLEEP QUALITY	HOW MANY HOURS DID YOU SLEEP?	DREAM NOTES
☐ GOOD		
☐ NEUTRAL	WHAT TIME DID YOU GO TO BED?	
☐ STRESSED	☐ AM ☐ PM	

SELF CARE TRACKER:

MIND / SPIRIT	EXERCISE / PHYSICAL ACTIVITY

DAILY JOURNAL

MEDITATION LOG

DATE	TIME	HOW LONG

MOOD TRACKER:

BEFORE	AFTER	THOUGHTS / NOTES ON YOUR MEDITATION
☐ GOOD	☐ GOOD	
☐ NEUTRAL	☐ NEUTRAL	
☐ STRESSED	☐ STRESSED	

SLEEP TRACKER:

SLEEP QUALITY	HOW MANY HOURS DID YOU SLEEP?	DREAM NOTES
☐ GOOD		
☐ NEUTRAL	WHAT TIME DID YOU GO TO BED?	
☐ STRESSED	☐ AM ☐ PM	

SELF CARE TRACKER:

MIND / SPIRIT	EXERCISE / PHYSICAL ACTIVITY

DAILY JOURNAL

MEDITATION LOG

DATE	TIME	HOW LONG

MOOD TRACKER:

BEFORE	AFTER	THOUGHTS / NOTES ON YOUR MEDITATION
☐ GOOD	☐ GOOD	
☐ NEUTRAL	☐ NEUTRAL	
☐ STRESSED	☐ STRESSED	

SLEEP TRACKER:

SLEEP QUALITY	HOW MANY HOURS DID YOU SLEEP?	DREAM NOTES
☐ GOOD		
☐ NEUTRAL	WHAT TIME DID YOU GO TO BED?	
☐ STRESSED	☐ AM ☐ PM	

SELF CARE TRACKER:

MIND / SPIRIT	EXERCISE / PHYSICAL ACTIVITY

DAILY JOURNAL

MEDITATION LOG

DATE	TIME	HOW LONG

MOOD TRACKER:

BEFORE	AFTER	THOUGHTS / NOTES ON YOUR MEDITATION
☐ GOOD	☐ GOOD	
☐ NEUTRAL	☐ NEUTRAL	
☐ STRESSED	☐ STRESSED	

SLEEP TRACKER:

SLEEP QUALITY	HOW MANY HOURS DID YOU SLEEP?	DREAM NOTES
☐ GOOD		
☐ NEUTRAL	WHAT TIME DID YOU GO TO BED?	
☐ STRESSED	☐ AM ☐ PM	

SELF CARE TRACKER:

MIND / SPIRIT	EXERCISE / PHYSICAL ACTIVITY

DAILY JOURNAL

MEDITATION LOG

DATE	TIME	HOW LONG

MOOD TRACKER:

BEFORE	AFTER	THOUGHTS / NOTES ON YOUR MEDITATION
☐ GOOD	☐ GOOD	
☐ NEUTRAL	☐ NEUTRAL	
☐ STRESSED	☐ STRESSED	

SLEEP TRACKER:

SLEEP QUALITY	HOW MANY HOURS DID YOU SLEEP?	DREAM NOTES
☐ GOOD		
☐ NEUTRAL	WHAT TIME DID YOU GO TO BED?	
☐ STRESSED	☐ AM ☐ PM	

SELF CARE TRACKER:

MIND / SPIRIT	EXERCISE / PHYSICAL ACTIVITY

DAILY JOURNAL

MEDITATION LOG

DATE		TIME		HOW LONG	

MOOD TRACKER:

BEFORE	AFTER	THOUGHTS / NOTES ON YOUR MEDITATION
☐ GOOD	☐ GOOD	
☐ NEUTRAL	☐ NEUTRAL	
☐ STRESSED	☐ STRESSED	

SLEEP TRACKER:

SLEEP QUALITY	HOW MANY HOURS DID YOU SLEEP?	DREAM NOTES
☐ GOOD		
☐ NEUTRAL	WHAT TIME DID YOU GO TO BED?	
☐ STRESSED	☐ AM ☐ PM	

SELF CARE TRACKER:

MIND / SPIRIT	EXERCISE / PHYSICAL ACTIVITY

DAILY JOURNAL

MEDITATION LOG

DATE	TIME	HOW LONG

MOOD TRACKER:

BEFORE	AFTER	THOUGHTS / NOTES ON YOUR MEDITATION
☐ GOOD	☐ GOOD	
☐ NEUTRAL	☐ NEUTRAL	
☐ STRESSED	☐ STRESSED	

SLEEP TRACKER:

SLEEP QUALITY	HOW MANY HOURS DID YOU SLEEP?	DREAM NOTES
☐ GOOD		
☐ NEUTRAL	WHAT TIME DID YOU GO TO BED?	
☐ STRESSED	☐ AM ☐ PM	

SELF CARE TRACKER:

MIND / SPIRIT	EXERCISE / PHYSICAL ACTIVITY

DAILY JOURNAL

MEDITATION LOG

DATE	TIME	HOW LONG

MOOD TRACKER:

BEFORE	AFTER	THOUGHTS / NOTES ON YOUR MEDITATION
☐ GOOD	☐ GOOD	
☐ NEUTRAL	☐ NEUTRAL	
☐ STRESSED	☐ STRESSED	

SLEEP TRACKER:

SLEEP QUALITY	HOW MANY HOURS DID YOU SLEEP?	DREAM NOTES
☐ GOOD		
☐ NEUTRAL	WHAT TIME DID YOU GO TO BED?	
☐ STRESSED	☐ AM ☐ PM	

SELF CARE TRACKER:

MIND / SPIRIT	EXERCISE / PHYSICAL ACTIVITY

DAILY JOURNAL

MEDITATION LOG

DATE	TIME	HOW LONG

MOOD TRACKER:

BEFORE	AFTER	THOUGHTS / NOTES ON YOUR MEDITATION
☐ GOOD	☐ GOOD	
☐ NEUTRAL	☐ NEUTRAL	
☐ STRESSED	☐ STRESSED	

SLEEP TRACKER:

SLEEP QUALITY	HOW MANY HOURS DID YOU SLEEP?	DREAM NOTES
☐ GOOD		
☐ NEUTRAL	WHAT TIME DID YOU GO TO BED?	
☐ STRESSED	☐ AM ☐ PM	

SELF CARE TRACKER:

MIND / SPIRIT	EXERCISE / PHYSICAL ACTIVITY

DAILY JOURNAL

MEDITATION LOG

DATE		TIME	HOW LONG

MOOD TRACKER:

BEFORE	AFTER	THOUGHTS / NOTES ON YOUR MEDITATION
☐ GOOD	☐ GOOD	
☐ NEUTRAL	☐ NEUTRAL	
☐ STRESSED	☐ STRESSED	

SLEEP TRACKER:

SLEEP QUALITY	HOW MANY HOURS DID YOU SLEEP?	DREAM NOTES
☐ GOOD		
☐ NEUTRAL	WHAT TIME DID YOU GO TO BED?	
☐ STRESSED	☐ AM ☐ PM	

SELF CARE TRACKER:

MIND / SPIRIT	EXERCISE / PHYSICAL ACTIVITY

DAILY JOURNAL

MEDITATION LOG

DATE	TIME	HOW LONG

MOOD TRACKER:

BEFORE	AFTER	THOUGHTS / NOTES ON YOUR MEDITATION
☐ GOOD	☐ GOOD	
☐ NEUTRAL	☐ NEUTRAL	
☐ STRESSED	☐ STRESSED	

SLEEP TRACKER:

SLEEP QUALITY	HOW MANY HOURS DID YOU SLEEP?	DREAM NOTES
☐ GOOD		
☐ NEUTRAL	WHAT TIME DID YOU GO TO BED?	
☐ STRESSED	☐ AM ☐ PM	

SELF CARE TRACKER:

MIND / SPIRIT	EXERCISE / PHYSICAL ACTIVITY

DAILY JOURNAL

MEDITATION LOG

| DATE | TIME | HOW LONG |
|---|---|---|//

MOOD TRACKER:

BEFORE	AFTER	THOUGHTS / NOTES ON YOUR MEDITATION
☐ GOOD	☐ GOOD	
☐ NEUTRAL	☐ NEUTRAL	
☐ STRESSED	☐ STRESSED	

SLEEP TRACKER:

SLEEP QUALITY	HOW MANY HOURS DID YOU SLEEP?	DREAM NOTES
☐ GOOD		
☐ NEUTRAL	WHAT TIME DID YOU GO TO BED?	
☐ STRESSED	☐ AM ☐ PM	

SELF CARE TRACKER:

MIND / SPIRIT	EXERCISE / PHYSICAL ACTIVITY

DAILY JOURNAL

MEDITATION LOG

DATE	TIME	HOW LONG

MOOD TRACKER:

BEFORE	AFTER	THOUGHTS / NOTES ON YOUR MEDITATION
☐ GOOD	☐ GOOD	
☐ NEUTRAL	☐ NEUTRAL	
☐ STRESSED	☐ STRESSED	

SLEEP TRACKER:

SLEEP QUALITY	HOW MANY HOURS DID YOU SLEEP?	DREAM NOTES
☐ GOOD		
☐ NEUTRAL	WHAT TIME DID YOU GO TO BED?	
☐ STRESSED	☐ AM ☐ PM	

SELF CARE TRACKER:

MIND / SPIRIT	EXERCISE / PHYSICAL ACTIVITY

DAILY JOURNAL

MEDITATION LOG

DATE		TIME		HOW LONG	

MOOD TRACKER:

BEFORE	AFTER	THOUGHTS / NOTES ON YOUR MEDITATION
☐ GOOD	☐ GOOD	
☐ NEUTRAL	☐ NEUTRAL	
☐ STRESSED	☐ STRESSED	

SLEEP TRACKER:

SLEEP QUALITY	HOW MANY HOURS DID YOU SLEEP?	DREAM NOTES
☐ GOOD		
☐ NEUTRAL	WHAT TIME DID YOU GO TO BED?	
☐ STRESSED	☐ AM ☐ PM	

SELF CARE TRACKER:

MIND / SPIRIT	EXERCISE / PHYSICAL ACTIVITY

DAILY JOURNAL

MEDITATION LOG

| DATE | TIME | HOW LONG |

MOOD TRACKER:

BEFORE	AFTER	THOUGHTS / NOTES ON YOUR MEDITATION
☐ GOOD	☐ GOOD	
☐ NEUTRAL	☐ NEUTRAL	
☐ STRESSED	☐ STRESSED	

SLEEP TRACKER:

SLEEP QUALITY	HOW MANY HOURS DID YOU SLEEP?	DREAM NOTES
☐ GOOD		
☐ NEUTRAL	WHAT TIME DID YOU GO TO BED?	
☐ STRESSED	☐ AM ☐ PM	

SELF CARE TRACKER:

MIND / SPIRIT	EXERCISE / PHYSICAL ACTIVITY

DAILY JOURNAL

MEDITATION LOG

DATE	TIME	HOW LONG

MOOD TRACKER:

BEFORE	AFTER	THOUGHTS / NOTES ON YOUR MEDITATION
☐ GOOD	☐ GOOD	
☐ NEUTRAL	☐ NEUTRAL	
☐ STRESSED	☐ STRESSED	

SLEEP TRACKER:

SLEEP QUALITY	HOW MANY HOURS DID YOU SLEEP?	DREAM NOTES
☐ GOOD		
☐ NEUTRAL	WHAT TIME DID YOU GO TO BED?	
☐ STRESSED	☐ AM ☐ PM	

SELF CARE TRACKER:

MIND / SPIRIT	EXERCISE / PHYSICAL ACTIVITY

DAILY JOURNAL

MEDITATION LOG

DATE	TIME	HOW LONG

MOOD TRACKER:

BEFORE	AFTER	THOUGHTS / NOTES ON YOUR MEDITATION
☐ GOOD	☐ GOOD	
☐ NEUTRAL	☐ NEUTRAL	
☐ STRESSED	☐ STRESSED	

SLEEP TRACKER:

SLEEP QUALITY	HOW MANY HOURS DID YOU SLEEP?	DREAM NOTES
☐ GOOD		
☐ NEUTRAL	WHAT TIME DID YOU GO TO BED?	
☐ STRESSED	☐ AM ☐ PM	

SELF CARE TRACKER:

MIND / SPIRIT	EXERCISE / PHYSICAL ACTIVITY

DAILY JOURNAL

MEDITATION LOG

DATE	TIME	HOW LONG

MOOD TRACKER:

BEFORE	AFTER	THOUGHTS / NOTES ON YOUR MEDITATION
☐ GOOD	☐ GOOD	
☐ NEUTRAL	☐ NEUTRAL	
☐ STRESSED	☐ STRESSED	

SLEEP TRACKER:

SLEEP QUALITY	HOW MANY HOURS DID YOU SLEEP?	DREAM NOTES
☐ GOOD		
☐ NEUTRAL	WHAT TIME DID YOU GO TO BED?	
☐ STRESSED	☐ AM ☐ PM	

SELF CARE TRACKER:

MIND / SPIRIT	EXERCISE / PHYSICAL ACTIVITY

DAILY JOURNAL

MEDITATION LOG

DATE	TIME	HOW LONG

MOOD TRACKER:

BEFORE	AFTER	THOUGHTS / NOTES ON YOUR MEDITATION
☐ GOOD	☐ GOOD	
☐ NEUTRAL	☐ NEUTRAL	
☐ STRESSED	☐ STRESSED	

SLEEP TRACKER:

SLEEP QUALITY	HOW MANY HOURS DID YOU SLEEP?	DREAM NOTES
☐ GOOD		
☐ NEUTRAL	WHAT TIME DID YOU GO TO BED?	
☐ STRESSED	☐ AM ☐ PM	

SELF CARE TRACKER:

MIND / SPIRIT	EXERCISE / PHYSICAL ACTIVITY

DAILY JOURNAL

MEDITATION LOG

DATE	TIME	HOW LONG

MOOD TRACKER:

BEFORE	AFTER	THOUGHTS / NOTES ON YOUR MEDITATION
☐ GOOD	☐ GOOD	
☐ NEUTRAL	☐ NEUTRAL	
☐ STRESSED	☐ STRESSED	

SLEEP TRACKER:

SLEEP QUALITY	HOW MANY HOURS DID YOU SLEEP?	DREAM NOTES
☐ GOOD		
☐ NEUTRAL	WHAT TIME DID YOU GO TO BED?	
☐ STRESSED	☐ AM ☐ PM	

SELF CARE TRACKER:

MIND / SPIRIT	EXERCISE / PHYSICAL ACTIVITY

DAILY JOURNAL

MEDITATION LOG

DATE	TIME	HOW LONG

MOOD TRACKER:

BEFORE	AFTER	THOUGHTS / NOTES ON YOUR MEDITATION
☐ GOOD	☐ GOOD	
☐ NEUTRAL	☐ NEUTRAL	
☐ STRESSED	☐ STRESSED	

SLEEP TRACKER:

SLEEP QUALITY	HOW MANY HOURS DID YOU SLEEP?	DREAM NOTES
☐ GOOD		
☐ NEUTRAL	WHAT TIME DID YOU GO TO BED?	
☐ STRESSED	☐ AM ☐ PM	

SELF CARE TRACKER:

MIND / SPIRIT	EXERCISE / PHYSICAL ACTIVITY

DAILY JOURNAL

MEDITATION LOG

DATE		TIME		HOW LONG	

MOOD TRACKER:

BEFORE	AFTER	THOUGHTS / NOTES ON YOUR MEDITATION
☐ GOOD	☐ GOOD	
☐ NEUTRAL	☐ NEUTRAL	
☐ STRESSED	☐ STRESSED	

SLEEP TRACKER:

SLEEP QUALITY	HOW MANY HOURS DID YOU SLEEP?	DREAM NOTES
☐ GOOD		
☐ NEUTRAL	WHAT TIME DID YOU GO TO BED?	
☐ STRESSED	☐ AM ☐ PM	

SELF CARE TRACKER:

MIND / SPIRIT	EXERCISE / PHYSICAL ACTIVITY

DAILY JOURNAL

MEDITATION LOG

DATE	TIME	HOW LONG

MOOD TRACKER:

BEFORE	AFTER	THOUGHTS / NOTES ON YOUR MEDITATION
☐ GOOD	☐ GOOD	
☐ NEUTRAL	☐ NEUTRAL	
☐ STRESSED	☐ STRESSED	

SLEEP TRACKER:

SLEEP QUALITY	HOW MANY HOURS DID YOU SLEEP?	DREAM NOTES
☐ GOOD		
☐ NEUTRAL	WHAT TIME DID YOU GO TO BED?	
☐ STRESSED	☐ AM ☐ PM	

SELF CARE TRACKER:

MIND / SPIRIT	EXERCISE / PHYSICAL ACTIVITY

DAILY JOURNAL

MEDITATION LOG

DATE	TIME	HOW LONG

MOOD TRACKER:

BEFORE	AFTER	THOUGHTS / NOTES ON YOUR MEDITATION
☐ GOOD	☐ GOOD	
☐ NEUTRAL	☐ NEUTRAL	
☐ STRESSED	☐ STRESSED	

SLEEP TRACKER:

SLEEP QUALITY	HOW MANY HOURS DID YOU SLEEP?	DREAM NOTES
☐ GOOD		
☐ NEUTRAL	WHAT TIME DID YOU GO TO BED?	
☐ STRESSED	☐ AM ☐ PM	

SELF CARE TRACKER:

MIND / SPIRIT	EXERCISE / PHYSICAL ACTIVITY

DAILY JOURNAL

MEDITATION LOG

DATE	TIME	HOW LONG

MOOD TRACKER:

BEFORE	AFTER	THOUGHTS / NOTES ON YOUR MEDITATION
☐ GOOD	☐ GOOD	
☐ NEUTRAL	☐ NEUTRAL	
☐ STRESSED	☐ STRESSED	

SLEEP TRACKER:

SLEEP QUALITY	HOW MANY HOURS DID YOU SLEEP?	DREAM NOTES
☐ GOOD		
☐ NEUTRAL	WHAT TIME DID YOU GO TO BED?	
☐ STRESSED	☐ AM ☐ PM	

SELF CARE TRACKER:

MIND / SPIRIT	EXERCISE / PHYSICAL ACTIVITY

DAILY JOURNAL

MEDITATION LOG

DATE		TIME		HOW LONG	

MOOD TRACKER:

BEFORE	AFTER	THOUGHTS / NOTES ON YOUR MEDITATION
☐ GOOD	☐ GOOD	
☐ NEUTRAL	☐ NEUTRAL	
☐ STRESSED	☐ STRESSED	

SLEEP TRACKER:

SLEEP QUALITY	HOW MANY HOURS DID YOU SLEEP?	DREAM NOTES
☐ GOOD		
☐ NEUTRAL	WHAT TIME DID YOU GO TO BED?	
☐ STRESSED	☐ AM ☐ PM	

SELF CARE TRACKER:

MIND / SPIRIT	EXERCISE / PHYSICAL ACTIVITY

DAILY JOURNAL

MEDITATION LOG

DATE	TIME	HOW LONG

MOOD TRACKER:

BEFORE	AFTER	THOUGHTS / NOTES ON YOUR MEDITATION
☐ GOOD	☐ GOOD	
☐ NEUTRAL	☐ NEUTRAL	
☐ STRESSED	☐ STRESSED	

SLEEP TRACKER:

SLEEP QUALITY	HOW MANY HOURS DID YOU SLEEP?	DREAM NOTES
☐ GOOD		
☐ NEUTRAL	WHAT TIME DID YOU GO TO BED?	
☐ STRESSED	☐ AM ☐ PM	

SELF CARE TRACKER:

MIND / SPIRIT	EXERCISE / PHYSICAL ACTIVITY

DAILY JOURNAL

MEDITATION LOG

DATE	TIME	HOW LONG

MOOD TRACKER:

BEFORE	AFTER	THOUGHTS / NOTES ON YOUR MEDITATION
☐ GOOD	☐ GOOD	
☐ NEUTRAL	☐ NEUTRAL	
☐ STRESSED	☐ STRESSED	

SLEEP TRACKER:

SLEEP QUALITY	HOW MANY HOURS DID YOU SLEEP?	DREAM NOTES
☐ GOOD		
☐ NEUTRAL	WHAT TIME DID YOU GO TO BED?	
☐ STRESSED	☐ AM ☐ PM	

SELF CARE TRACKER:

MIND / SPIRIT	EXERCISE / PHYSICAL ACTIVITY

DAILY JOURNAL

MEDITATION LOG

DATE	TIME	HOW LONG

MOOD TRACKER:

BEFORE	AFTER	THOUGHTS / NOTES ON YOUR MEDITATION
☐ GOOD	☐ GOOD	
☐ NEUTRAL	☐ NEUTRAL	
☐ STRESSED	☐ STRESSED	

SLEEP TRACKER:

SLEEP QUALITY	HOW MANY HOURS DID YOU SLEEP?	DREAM NOTES
☐ GOOD		
☐ NEUTRAL	WHAT TIME DID YOU GO TO BED?	
☐ STRESSED	☐ AM ☐ PM	

SELF CARE TRACKER:

MIND / SPIRIT	EXERCISE / PHYSICAL ACTIVITY

DAILY JOURNAL

MEDITATION LOG

DATE		TIME		HOW LONG	

MOOD TRACKER:

BEFORE	AFTER	THOUGHTS / NOTES ON YOUR MEDITATION
☐ GOOD	☐ GOOD	
☐ NEUTRAL	☐ NEUTRAL	
☐ STRESSED	☐ STRESSED	

SLEEP TRACKER:

SLEEP QUALITY	HOW MANY HOURS DID YOU SLEEP?	DREAM NOTES
☐ GOOD		
☐ NEUTRAL	WHAT TIME DID YOU GO TO BED?	
☐ STRESSED	☐ AM ☐ PM	

SELF CARE TRACKER:

MIND / SPIRIT	EXERCISE / PHYSICAL ACTIVITY

DAILY JOURNAL

MEDITATION LOG

DATE	TIME	HOW LONG

MOOD TRACKER:

BEFORE	AFTER	THOUGHTS / NOTES ON YOUR MEDITATION
☐ GOOD	☐ GOOD	
☐ NEUTRAL	☐ NEUTRAL	
☐ STRESSED	☐ STRESSED	

SLEEP TRACKER:

SLEEP QUALITY	HOW MANY HOURS DID YOU SLEEP?	DREAM NOTES
☐ GOOD		
☐ NEUTRAL	WHAT TIME DID YOU GO TO BED?	
☐ STRESSED	☐ AM ☐ PM	

SELF CARE TRACKER:

MIND / SPIRIT	EXERCISE / PHYSICAL ACTIVITY

DAILY JOURNAL

MEDITATION LOG

DATE	TIME	HOW LONG

MOOD TRACKER:

BEFORE	AFTER	THOUGHTS / NOTES ON YOUR MEDITATION
☐ GOOD	☐ GOOD	
☐ NEUTRAL	☐ NEUTRAL	
☐ STRESSED	☐ STRESSED	

SLEEP TRACKER:

SLEEP QUALITY	HOW MANY HOURS DID YOU SLEEP?	DREAM NOTES
☐ GOOD		
☐ NEUTRAL	WHAT TIME DID YOU GO TO BED?	
☐ STRESSED	☐ AM ☐ PM	

SELF CARE TRACKER:

MIND / SPIRIT	EXERCISE / PHYSICAL ACTIVITY

DAILY JOURNAL

MEDITATION LOG

DATE	TIME	HOW LONG

MOOD TRACKER:

BEFORE	AFTER	THOUGHTS / NOTES ON YOUR MEDITATION
☐ GOOD	☐ GOOD	
☐ NEUTRAL	☐ NEUTRAL	
☐ STRESSED	☐ STRESSED	

SLEEP TRACKER:

SLEEP QUALITY	HOW MANY HOURS DID YOU SLEEP?	DREAM NOTES
☐ GOOD		
☐ NEUTRAL	WHAT TIME DID YOU GO TO BED?	
☐ STRESSED	☐ AM ☐ PM	

SELF CARE TRACKER:

MIND / SPIRIT	EXERCISE / PHYSICAL ACTIVITY

DAILY JOURNAL

MEDITATION LOG

DATE	TIME	HOW LONG

MOOD TRACKER:

BEFORE	AFTER	THOUGHTS / NOTES ON YOUR MEDITATION
☐ GOOD	☐ GOOD	
☐ NEUTRAL	☐ NEUTRAL	
☐ STRESSED	☐ STRESSED	

SLEEP TRACKER:

SLEEP QUALITY	HOW MANY HOURS DID YOU SLEEP?	DREAM NOTES
☐ GOOD		
☐ NEUTRAL	WHAT TIME DID YOU GO TO BED?	
☐ STRESSED	☐ AM ☐ PM	

SELF CARE TRACKER:

MIND / SPIRIT	EXERCISE / PHYSICAL ACTIVITY

DAILY JOURNAL

MEDITATION LOG

DATE   TIME   HOW LONG

MOOD TRACKER:

BEFORE	AFTER	THOUGHTS / NOTES ON YOUR MEDITATION
☐ GOOD	☐ GOOD	
☐ NEUTRAL	☐ NEUTRAL	
☐ STRESSED	☐ STRESSED	

SLEEP TRACKER:

SLEEP QUALITY	HOW MANY HOURS DID YOU SLEEP?	DREAM NOTES
☐ GOOD		
☐ NEUTRAL	WHAT TIME DID YOU GO TO BED?	
☐ STRESSED	☐ AM ☐ PM	

SELF CARE TRACKER:

MIND / SPIRIT	EXERCISE / PHYSICAL ACTIVITY

DAILY JOURNAL

MEDITATION LOG

DATE		TIME		HOW LONG

MOOD TRACKER:

BEFORE	AFTER	THOUGHTS / NOTES ON YOUR MEDITATION
☐ GOOD	☐ GOOD	
☐ NEUTRAL	☐ NEUTRAL	
☐ STRESSED	☐ STRESSED	

SLEEP TRACKER:

SLEEP QUALITY	HOW MANY HOURS DID YOU SLEEP?	DREAM NOTES
☐ GOOD		
☐ NEUTRAL	WHAT TIME DID YOU GO TO BED?	
☐ STRESSED	☐ AM ☐ PM	

SELF CARE TRACKER:

MIND / SPIRIT	EXERCISE / PHYSICAL ACTIVITY

DAILY JOURNAL

MEDITATION LOG

DATE	TIME	HOW LONG

MOOD TRACKER:

BEFORE	AFTER	THOUGHTS / NOTES ON YOUR MEDITATION
☐ GOOD	☐ GOOD	
☐ NEUTRAL	☐ NEUTRAL	
☐ STRESSED	☐ STRESSED	

SLEEP TRACKER:

SLEEP QUALITY	HOW MANY HOURS DID YOU SLEEP?	DREAM NOTES
☐ GOOD		
☐ NEUTRAL	WHAT TIME DID YOU GO TO BED?	
☐ STRESSED	☐ AM ☐ PM	

SELF CARE TRACKER:

MIND / SPIRIT	EXERCISE / PHYSICAL ACTIVITY

DAILY JOURNAL

MEDITATION LOG

DATE	TIME	HOW LONG

MOOD TRACKER:

BEFORE	AFTER	THOUGHTS / NOTES ON YOUR MEDITATION
☐ GOOD	☐ GOOD	
☐ NEUTRAL	☐ NEUTRAL	
☐ STRESSED	☐ STRESSED	

SLEEP TRACKER:

SLEEP QUALITY	HOW MANY HOURS DID YOU SLEEP?	DREAM NOTES
☐ GOOD		
☐ NEUTRAL	WHAT TIME DID YOU GO TO BED?	
☐ STRESSED	☐ AM ☐ PM	

SELF CARE TRACKER:

MIND / SPIRIT	EXERCISE / PHYSICAL ACTIVITY

DAILY JOURNAL

MEDITATION LOG

DATE   TIME   HOW LONG

MOOD TRACKER:

BEFORE	AFTER	THOUGHTS / NOTES ON YOUR MEDITATION
☐ GOOD	☐ GOOD	
☐ NEUTRAL	☐ NEUTRAL	
☐ STRESSED	☐ STRESSED	

SLEEP TRACKER:

SLEEP QUALITY	HOW MANY HOURS DID YOU SLEEP?	DREAM NOTES
☐ GOOD		
☐ NEUTRAL	WHAT TIME DID YOU GO TO BED?	
☐ STRESSED	☐ AM ☐ PM	

SELF CARE TRACKER:

MIND / SPIRIT	EXERCISE / PHYSICAL ACTIVITY

DAILY JOURNAL

MEDITATION LOG

DATE		TIME		HOW LONG	

MOOD TRACKER:

BEFORE	AFTER		THOUGHTS / NOTES ON YOUR MEDITATION
☐ GOOD	☐ GOOD		
☐ NEUTRAL	☐ NEUTRAL		
☐ STRESSED	☐ STRESSED		

SLEEP TRACKER:

SLEEP QUALITY	HOW MANY HOURS DID YOU SLEEP?		DREAM NOTES
☐ GOOD			
☐ NEUTRAL	WHAT TIME DID YOU GO TO BED?		
☐ STRESSED		☐ AM ☐ PM	

SELF CARE TRACKER:

MIND / SPIRIT	EXERCISE / PHYSICAL ACTIVITY

DAILY JOURNAL

MEDITATION LOG

DATE	TIME	HOW LONG

MOOD TRACKER:

BEFORE	AFTER	THOUGHTS / NOTES ON YOUR MEDITATION
☐ GOOD	☐ GOOD	
☐ NEUTRAL	☐ NEUTRAL	
☐ STRESSED	☐ STRESSED	

SLEEP TRACKER:

SLEEP QUALITY	HOW MANY HOURS DID YOU SLEEP?	DREAM NOTES
☐ GOOD		
☐ NEUTRAL	WHAT TIME DID YOU GO TO BED?	
☐ STRESSED	☐ AM ☐ PM	

SELF CARE TRACKER:

MIND / SPIRIT	EXERCISE / PHYSICAL ACTIVITY

DAILY JOURNAL

MEDITATION LOG

DATE	TIME	HOW LONG

MOOD TRACKER:

BEFORE	AFTER	THOUGHTS / NOTES ON YOUR MEDITATION
☐ GOOD	☐ GOOD	
☐ NEUTRAL	☐ NEUTRAL	
☐ STRESSED	☐ STRESSED	

SLEEP TRACKER:

SLEEP QUALITY	HOW MANY HOURS DID YOU SLEEP?	DREAM NOTES
☐ GOOD		
☐ NEUTRAL	WHAT TIME DID YOU GO TO BED?	
☐ STRESSED	☐ AM ☐ PM	

SELF CARE TRACKER:

MIND / SPIRIT	EXERCISE / PHYSICAL ACTIVITY

DAILY JOURNAL

MEDITATION LOG

DATE   TIME   HOW LONG

MOOD TRACKER:

BEFORE	AFTER	THOUGHTS / NOTES ON YOUR MEDITATION
☐ GOOD	☐ GOOD	
☐ NEUTRAL	☐ NEUTRAL	
☐ STRESSED	☐ STRESSED	

SLEEP TRACKER:

SLEEP QUALITY	HOW MANY HOURS DID YOU SLEEP?	DREAM NOTES
☐ GOOD		
☐ NEUTRAL	WHAT TIME DID YOU GO TO BED?	
☐ STRESSED	☐ AM ☐ PM	

SELF CARE TRACKER:

MIND / SPIRIT	EXERCISE / PHYSICAL ACTIVITY

DAILY JOURNAL

MEDITATION LOG

DATE	TIME	HOW LONG

MOOD TRACKER:

BEFORE	AFTER	THOUGHTS / NOTES ON YOUR MEDITATION
☐ GOOD	☐ GOOD	
☐ NEUTRAL	☐ NEUTRAL	
☐ STRESSED	☐ STRESSED	

SLEEP TRACKER:

SLEEP QUALITY	HOW MANY HOURS DID YOU SLEEP?	DREAM NOTES
☐ GOOD		
☐ NEUTRAL	WHAT TIME DID YOU GO TO BED?	
☐ STRESSED	☐ AM ☐ PM	

SELF CARE TRACKER:

MIND / SPIRIT	EXERCISE / PHYSICAL ACTIVITY

DAILY JOURNAL

MEDITATION LOG

DATE	TIME	HOW LONG

MOOD TRACKER:

BEFORE	AFTER	THOUGHTS / NOTES ON YOUR MEDITATION
☐ GOOD	☐ GOOD	
☐ NEUTRAL	☐ NEUTRAL	
☐ STRESSED	☐ STRESSED	

SLEEP TRACKER:

SLEEP QUALITY	HOW MANY HOURS DID YOU SLEEP?	DREAM NOTES
☐ GOOD		
☐ NEUTRAL	WHAT TIME DID YOU GO TO BED?	
☐ STRESSED	☐ AM ☐ PM	

SELF CARE TRACKER:

MIND / SPIRIT	EXERCISE / PHYSICAL ACTIVITY

DAILY JOURNAL

MEDITATION LOG

DATE		TIME	HOW LONG

MOOD TRACKER:

BEFORE	AFTER	THOUGHTS / NOTES ON YOUR MEDITATION
☐ GOOD	☐ GOOD	
☐ NEUTRAL	☐ NEUTRAL	
☐ STRESSED	☐ STRESSED	

SLEEP TRACKER:

SLEEP QUALITY	HOW MANY HOURS DID YOU SLEEP?	DREAM NOTES
☐ GOOD		
☐ NEUTRAL	WHAT TIME DID YOU GO TO BED?	
☐ STRESSED	☐ AM ☐ PM	

SELF CARE TRACKER:

MIND / SPIRIT	EXERCISE / PHYSICAL ACTIVITY

DAILY JOURNAL

MEDITATION LOG

DATE	TIME	HOW LONG

MOOD TRACKER:

BEFORE	AFTER	THOUGHTS / NOTES ON YOUR MEDITATION
☐ GOOD	☐ GOOD	
☐ NEUTRAL	☐ NEUTRAL	
☐ STRESSED	☐ STRESSED	

SLEEP TRACKER:

SLEEP QUALITY	HOW MANY HOURS DID YOU SLEEP?	DREAM NOTES
☐ GOOD		
☐ NEUTRAL	WHAT TIME DID YOU GO TO BED?	
☐ STRESSED	☐ AM ☐ PM	

SELF CARE TRACKER:

MIND / SPIRIT	EXERCISE / PHYSICAL ACTIVITY

DAILY JOURNAL

MEDITATION LOG

DATE	TIME	HOW LONG

MOOD TRACKER:

BEFORE	AFTER	THOUGHTS / NOTES ON YOUR MEDITATION
☐ GOOD	☐ GOOD	
☐ NEUTRAL	☐ NEUTRAL	
☐ STRESSED	☐ STRESSED	

SLEEP TRACKER:

SLEEP QUALITY	HOW MANY HOURS DID YOU SLEEP?	DREAM NOTES
☐ GOOD		
☐ NEUTRAL	WHAT TIME DID YOU GO TO BED?	
☐ STRESSED	☐ AM ☐ PM	

SELF CARE TRACKER:

MIND / SPIRIT	EXERCISE / PHYSICAL ACTIVITY

DAILY JOURNAL

MEDITATION LOG

DATE	TIME	HOW LONG

MOOD TRACKER:

BEFORE	AFTER	THOUGHTS / NOTES ON YOUR MEDITATION
☐ GOOD	☐ GOOD	
☐ NEUTRAL	☐ NEUTRAL	
☐ STRESSED	☐ STRESSED	

SLEEP TRACKER:

SLEEP QUALITY	HOW MANY HOURS DID YOU SLEEP?	DREAM NOTES
☐ GOOD		
☐ NEUTRAL	WHAT TIME DID YOU GO TO BED?	
☐ STRESSED	☐ AM ☐ PM	

SELF CARE TRACKER:

MIND / SPIRIT	EXERCISE / PHYSICAL ACTIVITY

DAILY JOURNAL

MEDITATION LOG

DATE	TIME	HOW LONG

MOOD TRACKER:

BEFORE	AFTER	THOUGHTS / NOTES ON YOUR MEDITATION
☐ GOOD	☐ GOOD	
☐ NEUTRAL	☐ NEUTRAL	
☐ STRESSED	☐ STRESSED	

SLEEP TRACKER:

SLEEP QUALITY	HOW MANY HOURS DID YOU SLEEP?	DREAM NOTES
☐ GOOD		
☐ NEUTRAL	WHAT TIME DID YOU GO TO BED?	
☐ STRESSED	☐ AM ☐ PM	

SELF CARE TRACKER:

MIND / SPIRIT	EXERCISE / PHYSICAL ACTIVITY

DAILY JOURNAL

MEDITATION LOG

DATE   TIME   HOW LONG

MOOD TRACKER:

BEFORE	AFTER	THOUGHTS / NOTES ON YOUR MEDITATION
☐ GOOD	☐ GOOD	
☐ NEUTRAL	☐ NEUTRAL	
☐ STRESSED	☐ STRESSED	

SLEEP TRACKER:

SLEEP QUALITY	HOW MANY HOURS DID YOU SLEEP?	DREAM NOTES
☐ GOOD		
☐ NEUTRAL	WHAT TIME DID YOU GO TO BED?	
☐ STRESSED	☐ AM ☐ PM	

SELF CARE TRACKER:

MIND / SPIRIT	EXERCISE / PHYSICAL ACTIVITY

DAILY JOURNAL

MEDITATION LOG

DATE		TIME	HOW LONG

MOOD TRACKER:

BEFORE	AFTER	THOUGHTS / NOTES ON YOUR MEDITATION
☐ GOOD	☐ GOOD	
☐ NEUTRAL	☐ NEUTRAL	
☐ STRESSED	☐ STRESSED	

SLEEP TRACKER:

SLEEP QUALITY	HOW MANY HOURS DID YOU SLEEP?	DREAM NOTES
☐ GOOD		
☐ NEUTRAL	WHAT TIME DID YOU GO TO BED?	
☐ STRESSED	☐ AM ☐ PM	

SELF CARE TRACKER:

MIND / SPIRIT	EXERCISE / PHYSICAL ACTIVITY

DAILY JOURNAL

MEDITATION LOG

DATE	TIME	HOW LONG

MOOD TRACKER:

BEFORE	AFTER	THOUGHTS / NOTES ON YOUR MEDITATION
☐ GOOD	☐ GOOD	
☐ NEUTRAL	☐ NEUTRAL	
☐ STRESSED	☐ STRESSED	

SLEEP TRACKER:

SLEEP QUALITY	HOW MANY HOURS DID YOU SLEEP?	DREAM NOTES
☐ GOOD		
☐ NEUTRAL	WHAT TIME DID YOU GO TO BED?	
☐ STRESSED	☐ AM ☐ PM	

SELF CARE TRACKER:

MIND / SPIRIT	EXERCISE / PHYSICAL ACTIVITY

DAILY JOURNAL

MEDITATION LOG

DATE		TIME		HOW LONG	

MOOD TRACKER:

BEFORE	AFTER	THOUGHTS / NOTES ON YOUR MEDITATION
☐ GOOD	☐ GOOD	
☐ NEUTRAL	☐ NEUTRAL	
☐ STRESSED	☐ STRESSED	

SLEEP TRACKER:

SLEEP QUALITY	HOW MANY HOURS DID YOU SLEEP?	DREAM NOTES
☐ GOOD		
☐ NEUTRAL	WHAT TIME DID YOU GO TO BED?	
☐ STRESSED	☐ AM ☐ PM	

SELF CARE TRACKER:

MIND / SPIRIT	EXERCISE / PHYSICAL ACTIVITY

DAILY JOURNAL

MEDITATION LOG

DATE	TIME	HOW LONG

MOOD TRACKER:

BEFORE	AFTER	THOUGHTS / NOTES ON YOUR MEDITATION
☐ GOOD	☐ GOOD	
☐ NEUTRAL	☐ NEUTRAL	
☐ STRESSED	☐ STRESSED	

SLEEP TRACKER:

SLEEP QUALITY	HOW MANY HOURS DID YOU SLEEP?	DREAM NOTES
☐ GOOD		
☐ NEUTRAL	WHAT TIME DID YOU GO TO BED?	
☐ STRESSED	☐ AM ☐ PM	

SELF CARE TRACKER:

MIND / SPIRIT	EXERCISE / PHYSICAL ACTIVITY

DAILY JOURNAL

MEDITATION LOG

DATE	TIME	HOW LONG

MOOD TRACKER:

BEFORE	AFTER	THOUGHTS / NOTES ON YOUR MEDITATION
☐ GOOD	☐ GOOD	
☐ NEUTRAL	☐ NEUTRAL	
☐ STRESSED	☐ STRESSED	

SLEEP TRACKER:

SLEEP QUALITY	HOW MANY HOURS DID YOU SLEEP?	DREAM NOTES
☐ GOOD		
☐ NEUTRAL	WHAT TIME DID YOU GO TO BED?	
☐ STRESSED	☐ AM ☐ PM	

SELF CARE TRACKER:

MIND / SPIRIT	EXERCISE / PHYSICAL ACTIVITY

DAILY JOURNAL

MEDITATION LOG

DATE	TIME	HOW LONG

MOOD TRACKER:

BEFORE	AFTER	THOUGHTS / NOTES ON YOUR MEDITATION
☐ GOOD	☐ GOOD	
☐ NEUTRAL	☐ NEUTRAL	
☐ STRESSED	☐ STRESSED	

SLEEP TRACKER:

SLEEP QUALITY	HOW MANY HOURS DID YOU SLEEP?	DREAM NOTES
☐ GOOD		
☐ NEUTRAL	WHAT TIME DID YOU GO TO BED?	
☐ STRESSED	☐ AM ☐ PM	

SELF CARE TRACKER:

MIND / SPIRIT	EXERCISE / PHYSICAL ACTIVITY

DAILY JOURNAL

MEDITATION LOG

DATE	TIME	HOW LONG

MOOD TRACKER:

BEFORE	AFTER	THOUGHTS / NOTES ON YOUR MEDITATION
☐ GOOD	☐ GOOD	
☐ NEUTRAL	☐ NEUTRAL	
☐ STRESSED	☐ STRESSED	

SLEEP TRACKER:

SLEEP QUALITY	HOW MANY HOURS DID YOU SLEEP?	DREAM NOTES
☐ GOOD		
☐ NEUTRAL	WHAT TIME DID YOU GO TO BED?	
☐ STRESSED	☐ AM ☐ PM	

SELF CARE TRACKER:

MIND / SPIRIT	EXERCISE / PHYSICAL ACTIVITY

DAILY JOURNAL

MEDITATION LOG

DATE	TIME	HOW LONG

MOOD TRACKER:

BEFORE	AFTER	THOUGHTS / NOTES ON YOUR MEDITATION
☐ GOOD	☐ GOOD	
☐ NEUTRAL	☐ NEUTRAL	
☐ STRESSED	☐ STRESSED	

SLEEP TRACKER:

SLEEP QUALITY	HOW MANY HOURS DID YOU SLEEP?	DREAM NOTES
☐ GOOD		
☐ NEUTRAL	WHAT TIME DID YOU GO TO BED?	
☐ STRESSED	☐ AM ☐ PM	

SELF CARE TRACKER:

MIND / SPIRIT	EXERCISE / PHYSICAL ACTIVITY

DAILY JOURNAL

MEDITATION LOG

DATE		TIME		HOW LONG	

MOOD TRACKER:

BEFORE	AFTER	THOUGHTS / NOTES ON YOUR MEDITATION
☐ GOOD	☐ GOOD	
☐ NEUTRAL	☐ NEUTRAL	
☐ STRESSED	☐ STRESSED	

SLEEP TRACKER:

SLEEP QUALITY	HOW MANY HOURS DID YOU SLEEP?	DREAM NOTES
☐ GOOD		
☐ NEUTRAL	WHAT TIME DID YOU GO TO BED?	
☐ STRESSED	☐ AM ☐ PM	

SELF CARE TRACKER:

MIND / SPIRIT	EXERCISE / PHYSICAL ACTIVITY

DAILY JOURNAL

MEDITATION LOG

DATE	TIME	HOW LONG

MOOD TRACKER:

BEFORE	AFTER	THOUGHTS / NOTES ON YOUR MEDITATION
☐ GOOD	☐ GOOD	
☐ NEUTRAL	☐ NEUTRAL	
☐ STRESSED	☐ STRESSED	

SLEEP TRACKER:

SLEEP QUALITY	HOW MANY HOURS DID YOU SLEEP?	DREAM NOTES
☐ GOOD		
☐ NEUTRAL	WHAT TIME DID YOU GO TO BED?	
☐ STRESSED	☐ AM ☐ PM	

SELF CARE TRACKER:

MIND / SPIRIT	EXERCISE / PHYSICAL ACTIVITY

DAILY JOURNAL

MEDITATION LOG

DATE	TIME	HOW LONG

MOOD TRACKER:

BEFORE	AFTER	THOUGHTS / NOTES ON YOUR MEDITATION
☐ GOOD	☐ GOOD	
☐ NEUTRAL	☐ NEUTRAL	
☐ STRESSED	☐ STRESSED	

SLEEP TRACKER:

SLEEP QUALITY	HOW MANY HOURS DID YOU SLEEP?	DREAM NOTES
☐ GOOD		
☐ NEUTRAL	WHAT TIME DID YOU GO TO BED?	
☐ STRESSED	☐ AM ☐ PM	

SELF CARE TRACKER:

MIND / SPIRIT	EXERCISE / PHYSICAL ACTIVITY

DAILY JOURNAL

MEDITATION LOG

DATE	TIME	HOW LONG

MOOD TRACKER:

BEFORE	AFTER	THOUGHTS / NOTES ON YOUR MEDITATION
☐ GOOD	☐ GOOD	
☐ NEUTRAL	☐ NEUTRAL	
☐ STRESSED	☐ STRESSED	

SLEEP TRACKER:

SLEEP QUALITY	HOW MANY HOURS DID YOU SLEEP?	DREAM NOTES
☐ GOOD		
☐ NEUTRAL	WHAT TIME DID YOU GO TO BED?	
☐ STRESSED	☐ AM ☐ PM	

SELF CARE TRACKER:

MIND / SPIRIT	EXERCISE / PHYSICAL ACTIVITY

DAILY JOURNAL

MEDITATION LOG

DATE	TIME	HOW LONG

MOOD TRACKER:

BEFORE	AFTER	THOUGHTS / NOTES ON YOUR MEDITATION
☐ GOOD	☐ GOOD	
☐ NEUTRAL	☐ NEUTRAL	
☐ STRESSED	☐ STRESSED	

SLEEP TRACKER:

SLEEP QUALITY	HOW MANY HOURS DID YOU SLEEP?	DREAM NOTES
☐ GOOD		
☐ NEUTRAL	WHAT TIME DID YOU GO TO BED?	
☐ STRESSED	☐ AM ☐ PM	

SELF CARE TRACKER:

MIND / SPIRIT	EXERCISE / PHYSICAL ACTIVITY

DAILY JOURNAL

MEDITATION LOG

DATE	TIME	HOW LONG

MOOD TRACKER:

BEFORE	AFTER	THOUGHTS / NOTES ON YOUR MEDITATION
☐ GOOD	☐ GOOD	
☐ NEUTRAL	☐ NEUTRAL	
☐ STRESSED	☐ STRESSED	

SLEEP TRACKER:

SLEEP QUALITY	HOW MANY HOURS DID YOU SLEEP?	DREAM NOTES
☐ GOOD		
☐ NEUTRAL	WHAT TIME DID YOU GO TO BED?	
☐ STRESSED	☐ AM ☐ PM	

SELF CARE TRACKER:

MIND / SPIRIT	EXERCISE / PHYSICAL ACTIVITY

DAILY JOURNAL

MEDITATION LOG

DATE	TIME	HOW LONG

MOOD TRACKER:

BEFORE	AFTER	THOUGHTS / NOTES ON YOUR MEDITATION
☐ GOOD	☐ GOOD	
☐ NEUTRAL	☐ NEUTRAL	
☐ STRESSED	☐ STRESSED	

SLEEP TRACKER:

SLEEP QUALITY	HOW MANY HOURS DID YOU SLEEP?	DREAM NOTES
☐ GOOD		
☐ NEUTRAL	WHAT TIME DID YOU GO TO BED?	
☐ STRESSED	☐ AM ☐ PM	

SELF CARE TRACKER:

MIND / SPIRIT	EXERCISE / PHYSICAL ACTIVITY

DAILY JOURNAL

MEDITATION LOG

DATE	TIME	HOW LONG

MOOD TRACKER:

BEFORE	AFTER	THOUGHTS / NOTES ON YOUR MEDITATION
☐ GOOD	☐ GOOD	
☐ NEUTRAL	☐ NEUTRAL	
☐ STRESSED	☐ STRESSED	

SLEEP TRACKER:

SLEEP QUALITY	HOW MANY HOURS DID YOU SLEEP?	DREAM NOTES
☐ GOOD		
☐ NEUTRAL	WHAT TIME DID YOU GO TO BED?	
☐ STRESSED	☐ AM ☐ PM	

SELF CARE TRACKER:

MIND / SPIRIT	EXERCISE / PHYSICAL ACTIVITY

DAILY JOURNAL

MEDITATION LOG

DATE	TIME	HOW LONG

MOOD TRACKER:

BEFORE	AFTER	THOUGHTS / NOTES ON YOUR MEDITATION
☐ GOOD	☐ GOOD	
☐ NEUTRAL	☐ NEUTRAL	
☐ STRESSED	☐ STRESSED	

SLEEP TRACKER:

SLEEP QUALITY	HOW MANY HOURS DID YOU SLEEP?	DREAM NOTES
☐ GOOD		
☐ NEUTRAL	WHAT TIME DID YOU GO TO BED?	
☐ STRESSED	☐ AM ☐ PM	

SELF CARE TRACKER:

MIND / SPIRIT	EXERCISE / PHYSICAL ACTIVITY

DAILY JOURNAL

MEDITATION LOG

DATE	TIME	HOW LONG

MOOD TRACKER:

BEFORE	AFTER	THOUGHTS / NOTES ON YOUR MEDITATION
☐ GOOD	☐ GOOD	
☐ NEUTRAL	☐ NEUTRAL	
☐ STRESSED	☐ STRESSED	

SLEEP TRACKER:

SLEEP QUALITY	HOW MANY HOURS DID YOU SLEEP?	DREAM NOTES
☐ GOOD		
☐ NEUTRAL	WHAT TIME DID YOU GO TO BED?	
☐ STRESSED	☐ AM ☐ PM	

SELF CARE TRACKER:

MIND / SPIRIT	EXERCISE / PHYSICAL ACTIVITY

DAILY JOURNAL

MEDITATION LOG

DATE		TIME		HOW LONG	

MOOD TRACKER:

BEFORE	AFTER	THOUGHTS / NOTES ON YOUR MEDITATION
☐ GOOD	☐ GOOD	
☐ NEUTRAL	☐ NEUTRAL	
☐ STRESSED	☐ STRESSED	

SLEEP TRACKER:

SLEEP QUALITY	HOW MANY HOURS DID YOU SLEEP?	DREAM NOTES
☐ GOOD		
☐ NEUTRAL	WHAT TIME DID YOU GO TO BED?	
☐ STRESSED	☐ AM ☐ PM	

SELF CARE TRACKER:

MIND / SPIRIT	EXERCISE / PHYSICAL ACTIVITY

DAILY JOURNAL

MEDITATION LOG

DATE	TIME	HOW LONG

MOOD TRACKER:

BEFORE	AFTER	THOUGHTS / NOTES ON YOUR MEDITATION
☐ GOOD	☐ GOOD	
☐ NEUTRAL	☐ NEUTRAL	
☐ STRESSED	☐ STRESSED	

SLEEP TRACKER:

SLEEP QUALITY	HOW MANY HOURS DID YOU SLEEP?	DREAM NOTES
☐ GOOD		
☐ NEUTRAL	WHAT TIME DID YOU GO TO BED?	
☐ STRESSED	☐ AM ☐ PM	

SELF CARE TRACKER:

MIND / SPIRIT	EXERCISE / PHYSICAL ACTIVITY

DAILY JOURNAL

MEDITATION LOG

DATE	TIME	HOW LONG

MOOD TRACKER:

BEFORE	AFTER	THOUGHTS / NOTES ON YOUR MEDITATION
☐ GOOD	☐ GOOD	
☐ NEUTRAL	☐ NEUTRAL	
☐ STRESSED	☐ STRESSED	

SLEEP TRACKER:

SLEEP QUALITY	HOW MANY HOURS DID YOU SLEEP?	DREAM NOTES
☐ GOOD		
☐ NEUTRAL	WHAT TIME DID YOU GO TO BED?	
☐ STRESSED	☐ AM ☐ PM	

SELF CARE TRACKER:

MIND / SPIRIT	EXERCISE / PHYSICAL ACTIVITY

DAILY JOURNAL

MEDITATION LOG

DATE	TIME	HOW LONG

MOOD TRACKER:

BEFORE	AFTER	THOUGHTS / NOTES ON YOUR MEDITATION
☐ GOOD	☐ GOOD	
☐ NEUTRAL	☐ NEUTRAL	
☐ STRESSED	☐ STRESSED	

SLEEP TRACKER:

SLEEP QUALITY	HOW MANY HOURS DID YOU SLEEP?	DREAM NOTES
☐ GOOD		
☐ NEUTRAL	WHAT TIME DID YOU GO TO BED?	
☐ STRESSED	☐ AM ☐ PM	

SELF CARE TRACKER:

MIND / SPIRIT	EXERCISE / PHYSICAL ACTIVITY

DAILY JOURNAL

MEDITATION LOG

DATE	TIME	HOW LONG

MOOD TRACKER:

BEFORE	AFTER	THOUGHTS / NOTES ON YOUR MEDITATION
☐ GOOD	☐ GOOD	
☐ NEUTRAL	☐ NEUTRAL	
☐ STRESSED	☐ STRESSED	

SLEEP TRACKER:

SLEEP QUALITY	HOW MANY HOURS DID YOU SLEEP?	DREAM NOTES
☐ GOOD		
☐ NEUTRAL	WHAT TIME DID YOU GO TO BED?	
☐ STRESSED	☐ AM ☐ PM	

SELF CARE TRACKER:

MIND / SPIRIT	EXERCISE / PHYSICAL ACTIVITY

DAILY JOURNAL

MEDITATION LOG

DATE	TIME	HOW LONG

MOOD TRACKER:

BEFORE	AFTER	THOUGHTS / NOTES ON YOUR MEDITATION
☐ GOOD	☐ GOOD	
☐ NEUTRAL	☐ NEUTRAL	
☐ STRESSED	☐ STRESSED	

SLEEP TRACKER:

SLEEP QUALITY	HOW MANY HOURS DID YOU SLEEP?	DREAM NOTES
☐ GOOD		
☐ NEUTRAL	WHAT TIME DID YOU GO TO BED?	
☐ STRESSED	☐ AM ☐ PM	

SELF CARE TRACKER:

MIND / SPIRIT	EXERCISE / PHYSICAL ACTIVITY

DAILY JOURNAL

MEDITATION LOG

DATE	TIME	HOW LONG

MOOD TRACKER:

BEFORE	AFTER	THOUGHTS / NOTES ON YOUR MEDITATION
☐ GOOD	☐ GOOD	
☐ NEUTRAL	☐ NEUTRAL	
☐ STRESSED	☐ STRESSED	

SLEEP TRACKER:

SLEEP QUALITY	HOW MANY HOURS DID YOU SLEEP?	DREAM NOTES
☐ GOOD		
☐ NEUTRAL	WHAT TIME DID YOU GO TO BED?	
☐ STRESSED	☐ AM ☐ PM	

SELF CARE TRACKER:

MIND / SPIRIT	EXERCISE / PHYSICAL ACTIVITY

DAILY JOURNAL

MEDITATION LOG

DATE	TIME	HOW LONG

MOOD TRACKER:

BEFORE	AFTER	THOUGHTS / NOTES ON YOUR MEDITATION
☐ GOOD	☐ GOOD	
☐ NEUTRAL	☐ NEUTRAL	
☐ STRESSED	☐ STRESSED	

SLEEP TRACKER:

SLEEP QUALITY	HOW MANY HOURS DID YOU SLEEP?	DREAM NOTES
☐ GOOD		
☐ NEUTRAL	WHAT TIME DID YOU GO TO BED?	
☐ STRESSED	☐ AM ☐ PM	

SELF CARE TRACKER:

MIND / SPIRIT	EXERCISE / PHYSICAL ACTIVITY

DAILY JOURNAL

MEDITATION LOG

DATE	TIME	HOW LONG

MOOD TRACKER:

BEFORE	AFTER	THOUGHTS / NOTES ON YOUR MEDITATION
☐ GOOD	☐ GOOD	
☐ NEUTRAL	☐ NEUTRAL	
☐ STRESSED	☐ STRESSED	

SLEEP TRACKER:

SLEEP QUALITY	HOW MANY HOURS DID YOU SLEEP?	DREAM NOTES
☐ GOOD		
☐ NEUTRAL	WHAT TIME DID YOU GO TO BED?	
☐ STRESSED	☐ AM ☐ PM	

SELF CARE TRACKER:

MIND / SPIRIT	EXERCISE / PHYSICAL ACTIVITY

DAILY JOURNAL

MEDITATION LOG

DATE	TIME	HOW LONG

MOOD TRACKER:

BEFORE	AFTER	THOUGHTS / NOTES ON YOUR MEDITATION
☐ GOOD	☐ GOOD	
☐ NEUTRAL	☐ NEUTRAL	
☐ STRESSED	☐ STRESSED	

SLEEP TRACKER:

SLEEP QUALITY	HOW MANY HOURS DID YOU SLEEP?	DREAM NOTES
☐ GOOD		
☐ NEUTRAL	WHAT TIME DID YOU GO TO BED?	
☐ STRESSED	☐ AM ☐ PM	

SELF CARE TRACKER:

MIND / SPIRIT	EXERCISE / PHYSICAL ACTIVITY

DAILY JOURNAL

MEDITATION LOG

DATE		TIME		HOW LONG	

MOOD TRACKER:

BEFORE	AFTER	THOUGHTS / NOTES ON YOUR MEDITATION
☐ GOOD	☐ GOOD	
☐ NEUTRAL	☐ NEUTRAL	
☐ STRESSED	☐ STRESSED	

SLEEP TRACKER:

SLEEP QUALITY	HOW MANY HOURS DID YOU SLEEP?	DREAM NOTES
☐ GOOD		
☐ NEUTRAL	WHAT TIME DID YOU GO TO BED?	
☐ STRESSED	☐ AM ☐ PM	

SELF CARE TRACKER:

MIND / SPIRIT	EXERCISE / PHYSICAL ACTIVITY

DAILY JOURNAL